Carmen de la Cruz Iglesias

An analysis of market-orientated supply chain mani
with particular reference to the case of Zara

CU00729243

GRIN - Verlag für akademische Texte

Der GRIN Verlag mit Sitz in München hat sich seit der Gründung im Jahr 1998 auf die Veröffentlichung akademischer Texte spezialisiert.

Die Verlagswebseite www.grin.com ist für Studenten, Hochschullehrer und andere Akademiker die ideale Plattform, ihre Fachtexte, Studienarbeiten, Abschlussarbeiten oder Dissertationen einem breiten Publikum zu präsentieren.

Document Nr. V133008

Carmen de la Cruz Iglesias

# An analysis of market-orientated supply chain management in the retail fashion industry with particular reference to the case of Zara

GRIN Verlag

Bibliografische Information der Deutschen Nationalbibliothek: Die Deutsche Bibliothek
verzeichnet diese Publikation in der Deutschen Nationalbibliografie; detaillierte bibliografische Daten sind im Internet über http://dnb.d-nb.de/ abrufbar.

1. Auflage 2009
Copyright © 2009 GRIN Verlag GmbH
http://www.grin.com
Druck und Bindung: Books on Demand GmbH, Norderstedt Germany
ISBN 978-3-656-20914-0

# Business School

*An analysis of market-orientated supply chain management in the retail fashion industry with particular reference to the case of Zara*

**Abstract**

This paper has been developed to investigate how market orientation is aligned to supply chain management and thus, leverages a company's success. Answers were sought examining Zara, a strategic unit in the apparel Industria de Diseño Textil (Inditex) Group, which has widely been acknowledged as being a paradigmatic example of a leader in the fast fashion industry. Hereby, Zara's unique business model is investigated as well as its market-orientated approach that affects all scopes of its vertically integrated value chain. Finally, this report gives conclusions and an outlook while referring to the evaluated results.

# Table of Content

**Abbreviations:**

Inditex = Industria de Diseño Textil

H&M = Hennes and Mauritz

EDI = Electronic Data Interchange

## Table of Figures

## 1. Introduction

A glance at today's financial pages shows the consequences of economic recession. More and more retailers, such as Woolworth and Montgomery Ward, have become bankrupt as they were no longer good enough to compete for a customer's business. Or how Ander and Stern (2004, vii) describe it "They fell into the Black Hole of Retailing, the place where losing retailers go to die".

However, it has been widely acknowledged that an effective downstream-orientated supply chain, focused on cost reduction, can avoid this fate. Reduced costs lead to reduced prices and thus to satisfied customers. But that is only half the truth. There are other factors than stringent cost control that ensure business success. Supply chain management is not only about cost-efficiency rather than flexibility and adaptability. The faster a supply chain is able to respond to a market, the better the company's chances to achieve a competitive edge.

A paradigm for a company that manages to combine these aspects and to align its vertically integrated supply chain to the demands of its customers is Europe's fastest expanding international fashion retail group Industria de Diseño Textil with its workhorse Zara. Its unique integrated business model permeates the whole organization and provides evidence that market orientation paired with an outstanding supply chain management can be viewed as a key factor for success.

## 2. Aim and objectives

The aim of this report is to examine Zara's unique business model in relation to its market-orientated supply chain. In this framework certain questions are raised. For example, which elements of Zara's supply chain make it so unique? And related to this, how manages Zara to compete with other vertically integrated fashion retailers such as H&M and Benetton that use aggressive advertising to entice customers in their stores? Also, how does Zara integrate its market orientation in its supply chain? The present study will attempt to answer these and other questions. Research the success of Zara's market-orientated strategy as well as of its unconventional supply chain will help to figure out how they managed to become pioneer of fast fashion. To conclude, an outlook in Zara's future as well as the US market is provided.

# 3. Literature Review

## 3.1 The global fashion industry

In recent years, fashion retailers have proved to be the most promising and successful segment of international retailers (Fernie et al., 1997; Gereffi, 2005). However, the other side of the coin is that the clothing sector is also an extremely dynamic market. This can be traced back to the fact that the global fashion industry has changed considerably during the past decades. According to Mazaira et al. (2003, 220) a "democratization process of fashion" took place which made the market highly competitive. While fashion formerly used to be an elite consumption article, often linked with haute couture brands such as Gucci and Dior, it is now mass product like everything else. Mazaira et al. (2003) consider this broadening of the target market as the main reason for increased expectations of fashion retailers. According to them, fashion retailers have to maximize their speed and at the same time keep prices low. Walters (2006) argues contrariwise, blaming fast fashion retailers for this ephemerality. He states that the fast fashion retailers "[…] have influenced consumer expectations for speed, variety and style at low prices and have found it necessary to make changes to speed up the production cycle" (Walters, 2006, 86).

No matter who is taken into account, fact is that today's consumers are more demanding and fashion-conscious than they were before (The Economist, 2003). The fashion market therefore is not only characterized by non-influenceable factors such as weather and seasonal variation, but also by an ever-changing taste of customers who always want to be in vogue. This is confirmed by the definition of fashion that describes the fashion industry as a very volatile one: Fashion is "[..] a broad term that typically encompasses any product or market where there is an element of style that is likely to be short-lived" (Christopher at al., 2004, 367). For the companies this entails difficulties in making reliable forecasts. They have to develop flexible business models that enable them to react quickly to emerging trends.

Due to this fact, fast fashion retailers such as Custo Barcelona or Caramelo, spring up like mushrooms. And also more established fast fashion retailers such as the Swedish Hennes & Mauritz (H&M), the Spanish Mango or the Italian Benetton expand with vertiginous speed. Tokatli (2008) observes that "[T]there is now a race between a significant number of 'fast fashion' retailers to increase the number of their stores while maximizing the speed,

synchronicity and responsiveness of their supply chains" (Tokatli, 2008, 23). Thus, the question with regard to an adequate business strategy, that is able to withstand or even better adjust to these market turbulences, arises.

## 3.2 Market orientation

There are several options for a company to succeed in business. However, one of the most promising ones is to pursue a market-orientated strategy. According to Singh and Ranchhod (2004, 137) market orientation can be defined as a "set of activities coordinated in such a way that derives customer satisfaction through superior performance of products [...] while still being competitive [...] in the market place". A company implementing a market-orientated approach gives the customer's interests and the fulfillment of them top priority. The market orientation theory suggests that the efficient and effective creation of superior value for customers through understanding and satisfying their needs is the only way to achieve a competitive edge (Day 1994; Narver and Slater, 1990).

And although there are several studies that examine the impact of market orientation on business performance (Langerak et al., 2004, Mazaira et al., 2003; Hussein and Al-Hour, 2009) only few explain how to implement a market-orientated approach. Besides, most see the responsibility of the execution of marketing goals in the marketing department alone. However, as market orientation is more than a simple marketing strategy, every department should be involved (Mazaira et al., 2003). Therefore, a clear focus on creating superior value for the customer should permeate the entire company.

## 3.3 The merger of market orientation and supply chain management

To achieve an organisation-wide customer focus, the company needs to integrate all market-orientated activities adequately in its supply chain (Christopher et al., 2004). Thereby, logistics are a crucial factor to create a market-orientated firm and can be viewed as an advocate of cross-functional supply chain activities (Bowersox et al., 2003). Fernie (1994) argues that also quick response within supply chain management has gained much attention to realize a firm's market-orientated strategy. However, as a conclusion one can say that only an integrated market approach that synchronizes supply chain management with the entire process in the supply chain is able to deliver flexible response to customers' needs and wants. Notwithstanding such logical fit between supply chain management and market orientation, it

is still a big challenge for fashion companies to gain a sustainable competitive advantage within their limited scope of possibilities within the fashion process (Nobukaza et al., 2004). However, the Spanish fashion retailer Zara demonstrated that this is not impossible. Their whole business system is characterized by highly vertically integrated activites and extremely short lead times. And although Zara does not even have a "formalized" marketing department, they are nevertheless - or perhaps for exactly that reason - often taken as an example for a market-orientated company (Mazaira et al., 2003).

## 4.    Inditex - Zara

### 4.1    Background information

Zara was founded by Amancio Ortega Gaona in the Galician seaport A Coruña in 1975 (Inditex, 2008a). Henceforward, Zara with its parent Inditex, experienced an unprecedented success story. Its heavily oversubscribed stock price in May 2001 and an increase by nearly 50% in the year after pushed its market value to €13.4 billion and made his founder Ortega, to Spain's richest man (Ghemawat and Nueno, 2006). Today (FY 2008), the Inditex Group is represented with more than 4000 stores in 73 countries and employs nearly 90,000 people. The group had a net income of €1253 million and a gross profit of €5914 million. In addition to Zara (and Zara Kiddy's Class), Inditex owns seven other chains: Pull and Bear, Massimo Dutti, Bershka, Stradivarius, Oysho, Zara Home and the newly-founded format Uterqüe (Appendix I). In 2008, Inditex' powerhorse Zara had net sales of €6824 million, an increase of 25% compared to its fiscal year 2007. Zara accounted for 75% of the group's turnover in 2008 (Inditex 2009a). With 1292 stores worldwide, Zara expanded so rapidly that they managed to overtake the world's number one fashion retailer Gap (Keely and Clark, 2008).

### 4.2    Competitors

Besides competing with local retailers, national and international department stores or companies on the Internet, Inditex or Zara's major international competitors respectively - in terms of market - share are H&M, Benetton and Gap (Mazaira et al., 2003). Besides, Mango, Benetton, Adolfo Dominguez, Cortefiel, C&A and Next are also often mentioned as competitors. In addition, there are companies which distribute fashion as well as other products, such as El Corte Inglés and Carrefour. To give an idea of Zara's main competitors, a snapshot of H&M, Gap as well as Benetton is provided.

General information about Zara's key competitors

**H&M**

Hennes and Mauritz (H&M) was founded in 1947 in Sweden and offers middle-priced fashion for men, women, teenagers and children as well as cosmetics and accessories. Although H&M is considered as Inditex' closest competitor, there are several significant differences between these two retailers. First of all, H&M operates a single format and tends to have slightly lower prices than Zara. This might be due to the fact that H&M outsourced half of its production to low-wage countries (the other half to European suppliers). In contrast to Zara, H&M's expansion strategy is characterized by entering one country at a time. This led to the fact that Zara, albeit H&M started selling outside its home country ten years earlier, has a wider international presence. To entice customers in their stores, H&M hires celebrity designers such as Karl Lagerfeld and relies on extensive advertising. In contrast to Zara, H&M employs fewer designers and they refurbish their stores less frequently. H&M has 1,700 stores spread over 34 markets, with Germany being its biggest market (H&M, 2009).

**Gap**

Gap, incorporated in 1969 in San Francisco, was the world's largest specialist clothing retailer until it was bridged by Zara. The company sells clothing, personal care products and accessories at moderate price points. Gap's internationalization process is based on only a few countries. Having operated in the home market for nearly 20 years, Gap opened its stores in the UK and Canada (1987 and 1989). In the 1990s, Gap expanded into France and Japan. Gap outsourced 90% of its production, operations remain US-centric. Likewise Inditex, Gap has five different store chains, namely Gap, BananaRepublic, Old Navy, Piperlime. Altogether, Gap is represented with 3,100 stores in 6 countries: United States, Canada, the United Kingdom, France, Ireland and Japan. Gap outsourced all its production from suppliers in the US and abroad. To regain lost market shares and to further expand their product range, Gap acquired Athleta, which offers women's sportswear (Gap, 2009).

**Benetton**

Established in 1965 in Italy, Benetton became famous for offering brightly colored knitwear. In the 1980s and 1990s, its unconventional advertising helped the company to become famous. Today, the Benetton Group is present with 5,500 stores in 120 countries around the world. Besides its casual United Colors of Benetton, it is present through the glamour-orientated Sisley, the American college style-orientated Playlife and the streetwear range Killer Loop. These chains are mainly managed by independent partners and generate a total turnover of about 2 billion euro. Similar to Zara, Benetton has own manufacturing facilities and outsources only labor-intensive activities to subcontractors. However, more than 90% of the production is carried out in Europe. It is now controlled by Edizione Holding, the holding company of the Benetton family, with a 67% stake (Benetton, 2009).

**Figure 1: Competitor snapshot**

## 4.3    Zara's product range

Zara's range of product includes medium quality garments for women, men and kids. Furthermore, they offer shoes, accessories, toiletries, and cosmetics. More than 11,000 styles of garments are created each year (Ghemawat and Nueno, 2006; Tokatli, 2008). Zara provides its young customers (17-22 year old) with a great variety of up-to-date and well-designed styles at reasonable prices (Walters, 2006). The company uses its brand name to market different product lines, such as Zara Basic, Zara Women or Zara Trafaluc. All stores have the same range of products as the main idea is "that national borders are no impediment to sharing a single fashion culture" (Inditex, 2009b). Zara's products are affordable as well as fashionable. They can be settled between causal and formal, fresh and innovative (Appendix II).

However, Zara needs to be investigated further to establish differences in any other vertically integrated fashion retailers. Therefore, it is important to closely examine and elaborate Zara's value chain. In the following the single constituents of the supply chain (design and raw material sourcing, production and logistics, distribution and store sales) are described. In the end, everything is put in a nutshell.

# 5. Zara's market-orientated supply chain management

## 5.1 Design and raw material sourcing

Essential to Zara's market-orientated strategy is its vertically integrated supply chain, of which the first part is shown in figure 1:

**Figure 2: Design and raw material sourcing**

Zara's value chain starts and ends with the customer as main component of their market-orientated strategy (see page 15). The customers provide Zara with ideas for new styles. Designers walk along the streets and go to discos in order to take cues from the mainstream consumer (Reinach, 2005). Furthermore, trend-spotters surf the internet and travel the world to get a feel for the latest trends (Tokatli, 2008).

*"We don't invent trends, we follow them. [...] But we need to know what the trends are, so we follow them through magazines, fashion shows, movies and city streets. [...] We keep our eyes open"*

(Inditex press officer, quoted in Tungate, 2005, 52)

In addition, Zara's store managers constantly report what sells and what customer want (Mazaira et al., 2003; Tokatli, 2008). Unlike their competitors, Zara focuses on the market and therefore only develops styles if there is clear evidence of customer demand. If customers ask for a particular color or style, the shop manager informs the company and the style can be delivered in less than two weeks (Prahalad and Ramaswamy, 2004). They enter the relevant data in 'Cassiopeia', a system made for placing orders and for materializing requests quickly (Mazaira, 2003). The feedback is collected from the stores worldwide and then sent to Zara's commercial group and design department in real-time (Inditex, 2007). Unlike Gap, each store purchases on its own which leads to a different choice of products from store to store. Having put the request, a marketing team immediately starts to develop the styles, based on garment availability and regional sales pattern as well as on predictions about what will sell in each single market. In this first part of the value chain real-time systems seem to be a decisive

element as they facilitate the collaboration between customers, shop managers and designers and thus, help Zara to be up to speed with regard to latest trends and tastes. The customer is incorporated from the very beginning of the supply chain. But also downstream activities are permeated by a clear customer focus as it is discussed below.

The next step of Zara's supply chain is the raw material buying and finishing. The booking of most of the fabric is carried out by a 100%-owned subsidiary of Inditex, called Comditel. This company works together with about 200 suppliers of raw materials and fabrics and manages the entire finishing of the fabrics (Ghemawata and Nueno, 2006).

At the beginning of a season, an in-house design team prepares a range of drafts that serve as platform for the models that will eventually be launched. Having spotted the latest fashion trends, another team of designers makes final adaption to these models from the portfolio and thus, creates about 1,000 styles each month (Lincoln and Thomassen, 2008). In total, a team of 200 designers develops astonishing 11,000 new items every year compared with 2,000 – 4,000 products for Zara's key competitors H&M and Gap (Ghemawat and Nueno, 2006; Tokatli, 2008). Tight integration allows them to quickly use market-level information to create new designs and to feed them to manufacturing without delay. "Unlike companies that sequester their design staffs, Zara's cadre of 200 designers sits right in the midst of the production process" (Ferdows et al., 2004, 107). In the end, Zara has the choice between nearly 30,000 designs a year. However, 11,000 designs are selected and divided into 12-16 collections (Tokatli, 2008).

Before moving further in the value chain, it is important to decide whether the design can be produced and sold at a profit. Here, too, Zara follows a market-based approach. In contrast to other fashion retailers, that determine a price according to what they spent plus a target margin, Zara prices to market. This means that the sales department chooses a price in each country that equates marginal revenue to marginal costs of the material, production and suppliers in the particular country (Bonache and Cerviño, 1996; Mazaira et al., 2003). As materials and suppliers are chosen according to the price fixed before, prices mirror the market's willingness to pay (Mazaira et al., 2003). The fact that production costs are tailored to respond to customers needs, leads to a different positioning for Zara in emerging markets. While most people in Spain can afford Zara, the same brand in Mexico is only bought by people who earn good money. CEO Castellano explains it as follows:

*In Spain, with the prices we have and the information available to the public, about 80% of Spanish citizens can afford Zara. When we go to Mexico, for cultural reasons, for informational reasons, for economic reasons – because the average income in Mexico is $14,000 – our targeted customer base is narrower. Who buys from us in Mexico? The upper class and the middle class. [...] In Mexico we are targeting 14 million inhabitants, compared to 35-36 million in Spain [out of populations of 100 million and 40 million, respectively].*

(CEO Jose María Castellano, cited in Ghemawat and Nueno, 2006, 20)

Consequently, the prices of Zara's garments differ from country to country. Prices in Spain are the base of this scale of prices and therefore, the lowest in Europe D'Andrea and Arnold, 2002). For instance, a t-shirt product in Spain could be priced for €20 and the same product in the USA would cost more than €40 (a table of prices of a t-shirt at Zara is shown in Appendix III). Due to longer distribution channels, prices in international markets are generally higher (Ghemawat and Nueno, 2006).

After manufacturing a sample, every product is tested among a certain number of key stores (Ferdows et al., 2004). Only unambiguously winners are scheduled for mass-production. This is why failure rates of new products are reported to be only 1% compared to an industry average of 10% (Ghemawat and Nueno, 2006). Roughly one half of the cloth arrives undyed, so that Zara postpone colors when they know what is trendy (Coughlan et al., 2006; Tokatli, 2008; Walters, 2006). To allow these last-minute changes and thus, to remain flexible, Zara has its own dyeing company. Outside the distribution centre, the fabric is cut and dyed by robots in 23 highly automated factories. Due to its high dregree of vertical integration, Zara can manufacture 40% of its own fabric and purchases most dyes from its own subsidiaries (Ghemawat and Nueno, 2006)

## 5.2    Production and Logistics

Figure 3: Production and logistics

Having cut the fabrics company-owned trucks bring them, attached some sewing instructions, to outsourced workshops close to Inditex' factories where they are sewn (Heller, 2001). These 450 workshops are located in Northern Portugal and Galicia and perform labour- as well as scale intense sewing activities (Ghemawat and Nueno, 2006). As all of them subcontractors are in the proximity of Zara's main headquarters, their operations are closely monitored to ensure adherence to the tight production schedule (Ferdows et al., 2004). After sewing the garments, they are collected again and brought back to Zara's factory. There, products are washed, ironed, packed and ticketed within 10-15 days and with an average of 7 to 8 days before being sent on to the different distribution centres in Spain (Ferdows et al., 2004). According to Inditex, 63% of the group's production is carried out in European countries and Morocco, while 35% was carried out in Asia and 2% in other regions (Inditex 2008b). As large batches of cloth are produced in-house or Europe respectively, Inditex is less vulnerable to criticism in terms of sweatshop activities.

## 5.3    Distribution and store sales

Figure 4: Distribution and store sales

Zara's five-story distribution centre is among the world's largest warehouses with a size of 500,000m$^2$ (Ferdows et al., 2004; Helft, 2002). It is equipped with 200 km[1] of so-called UPS rails that assist in the production process. UPS is a conveyor system which is able to transfer garments overhead around the factory (Walters, 2006). It is connected to 14 factories through tunnels, each with overhead monorails that transport clothes on hangers to the warehouse. In

---

[1] roughly 124 miles

the warehouse, clothes get sorted and stored (Ferdows et al., 2004). The finished products are brought to Zara's logistic centres that are located all over Spain (see Figure 1). From there, products are delivered to the stores worldwide. Zara system is said to be capable to handle 40,000 items each hour (Tagliabue, 2003).

In 2001, the distribution center handled 130 million items, whereof three-fourths of these pieces were sent to stores in Europe (Ferdows et al., 2004). Additional, smaller satellite warehouses in Brazil, Argentina, and Mexico, consolidate ship-

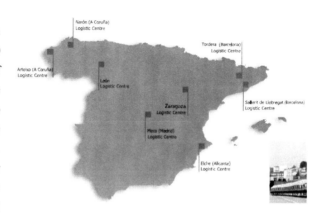

**Figure 5: Inditex distribution centre (Inditex 2008a)**

ments from Spain (Ferdows et al., 2004). Most of the products do not stay there longer than 72 hours. Company-owned trucks deliver the cloth to stores that can be reached overnight; cargo flights serve all farther destinations. Both, trucks and airfreights run on established schedules, similar to bus plans. Store deliveries are completed within, on average 24 for Europe and a maximum of 48 hours for Asia and America (Tagliabue, 2003; Tokatli, 2008). Hereby, distribution is 98.9% accurate with a shrinkage rate[2] of less than 0.5 per cent (Coughlan et al., 2006; Ferdows et al., 2004, Kumar and Linguri, 2006; McAfee and Sjoman, 2004). As Zara always sticks to this rigid shipping schedule, customers know exactly when the Zara stores are restocked (Coughlan et al., 2006).

At the end of FY2008, there were 4264 stores, 543 of them franchised (Inditex, 2099a). Most of them can be found in the world's priciest streets such as New York's 5th Avenue, Tokyo's Ginza or Milan's Corso Vittorio Emmanuele (see figure 5).

---

[2] shrinkage is the loss of inventory due to theft or damage

Figure 6: Zara's exquisite locations
all over the world (Inditex 2008a)

And although Zara belongs to middle-priced brands, its stores convey the image of a luxurious and expensive brand (Tungate, 2005). They are large and there is plenty of space between the different racks. Music, temperature and layout of the stores are evaluated regularly by mystery shoppers, thereby constantly adapting to market demands (Monllor, 2001). The same applies to Zara's shop windows. Alberto Figa, director of a Spanish a retailing industry consulting firm, explains "Their prices are low, but they present the products as if they were upscale [...] There isn't much difference between an Armani and a Zara window" (Figa, cited in Fuchs, 2007). Or as Kumar and Steenkamp (2007, 39) put it: "For Zara, the store window display is the major vehicle for advertising to the consumer. The windows, refreshed every two weeks, are large and dramatic, and feature the merchandise as a star".

This is why Zara does not think much of traditional advertising such as tv spots or advertising in fashion magazines. They rather rely on their stores as a main marketing platform. A strong focus on the interior of the stores and pivotal locations are Zara's prime marketing strategy (Ghemawat and Nueno, 2006; Kumar and Linguri, 2006). People enjoy shopping at Zara so that

they tell their friends about it. Instead of paying a lot of money for advertising, the company heavily relies on word of mouth. Compared to other fashion retailers such as H&M and Benetton, that spend an average of 3.5% of their revenue in advertising their products, Zara only spends 0.3% (Coughlan et al., 2006; Ghemawat and Nueno, 2006). And although the company does not have a "formalized marketing department" (Mazaira et al., 2003, 223), the American magazine advertising Age included Zara in the 50 companies with the most brilliant marketing strategies 2006 (AdAge, 2006).

According to Coughlan et al., 2006, a shopper in London visits a Zara store 17 times a year, whereas the same shopper visits a standard clothing store only four times per year. But how manages Zara to entice customers to their stores without any advertising? The secret lies in the creation of scarcity. A director of Inditex explains: "We want our customers to understand that if they like something, they must buy it now, because it won't be in the shops the following week" (Blanc, cited in Ghemawat and Nueno, 2006, 13). Thus, the company only produces batches of clothing in small quantities so that stores are restocked with new articles several times each week (Coughlan et al., 2006; Mazaira et al., 2003). If a product is not successful it is immediately taken off the store (Mazaira et al., 2003). In this way, losses in terms of fashion faux pas can be minimized. Shop managers in South Europe set their orders twice a week, "by 3:00 pm Wednesday and 6:00 pm Saturday. The other shops around the world place their orders by 3:00 pm Tuesday and 6:00 Friday" (Ferdows et al., 2004, 107). Again everything follows a precise rhythm. Strict adherence to these time lines make it possible that new styles are "whisk[ed] into stores with breathtaking speed" (Tungate, 2005, 50) and that an agile response to fashion trends can be ensured. Most items turnover in less than 1 week (Coughlan et al., 2006).

Customers perceive this and are therefore encouraged to visit the stores frequently (Mazaira et al., 2003). According to the CEO of the National Retail Federation, visiting a Zara shop as if you would "walk into a new store every two weeks" (Helft, 2002). As clothes are ironed, packed on hangers, equipped with security and price tags and put on shelf in advance. Zara's store managers simply put them on the display when they are delivered (Ferdows et al., 2004). The saved time is used is for value-added functions like customer service.

Another advantage of producing small batches is that Zara does not need to markdown merchandise as much as others do (Tokalti, 2008). "A study by Bain & Co. estimated the

industry average markdown ratio at approximately 50 per cent, and also found that fast fashion retailers sold only 15 per cent on sale" (Sull and Turconi, 2008, 4). Therefore, Zara is able to collect 85% of its list prices on its clothing while the industry average is 60-70% (Tokatli, 2008).

Thus we come full circle, returning to the customer at the end of this market-driven global chain. The customer is what keeps Zara's business running. Or is it the other way round?

## 5.4   Results

*"It's just got faster and faster, spinning not entirely out of control but certainly spinning at a rate that can make you dizzy"*

BBC quoting Hilary Alexander (BBC, 2004)

The success of Zara can be traced back to many different factors. While Mossingkoff and Stockert (2008) ascribe it to the company's seamless EDI implementation, Mazaira et al. (2003) view Zara's marketing strategy as a main factor for success. However, Coughlan et al. (2006, 389) state that "Zara's formula for success rests upon centralized control all the way through from its input sourcing (dyes, fabrics), to design, to logistics and shipping, and finally to retailing". However, most argue that Zara's performance can be traced back to its seemingly unbeatable speed (Appendix IV and V). Case studies reveal that Zara is able to operate on a lead-time of less than 15 days (D'Andrea and Arnold, 2002; Walters, 2006) whereas competitors like Gap need a lead-time of approximately 3 to 9 months (Ghemawat and Nueno, 2006). This "from sheep to shop" approach makes Zara astonishing twelve times faster than Gap, which only offers one tenth of all the products Zara does (Heft, 2002). But this is not the only aspect that distinguishes Zara from other fashion retailers. While its competitors focus on outsourcing, Zara manufactures nearly half oft its products on its own. Despite raising output in the factories, Zara's capacities consciously remain unused; instead of seeking for economies of scale, Zara produces small batches. And despite relying on external partners, the company manages design, storage, distribution and logistics on its own. Seamless communication helps that designer as well as production scheduler know what customers want and what they buy. According to the founder Ortega, fast fashion retailers namely have "five fingers touching the factory and five fingers touching the customer" (Amancio Ortega, cited in Ferdows et al., 2004).

Appendix VI shows the different elements of Zara's business system. Starting with corporate areas such as IT, Corporate Governance, Human Resources and International Management to product areas such as production, logistics, and merchandising, everything interacts and interlocks precisely as the cog wheels in a clockwork. And the most important cog in this clock is the customer. According to Inditex the customer even is the main reason for the group's existence. "[...] Inditex has given the customer an active role from the start of the chain and turned it into the principal drive for its entire business model" (Inditex, 2008b, 20). Zara always seems to move in step with its customers expectations. Walters (2006, 87) puts these value expectations of customers in an order according to importance to customers:

1. current fashion designs
2. immediate availability of fashion trends
3. variety/choice, low price with commensurate quality, service that includes "coordination ideas" and attractive
4. and functional store design.

Zara answers to these requirements with unconventional and to some extent even contradictory practices. The following summarizes Zara's main keys of success compared to other vertically integrated fashion retailers (see also Appendix VII and VII):

- inimitably short lead-times
- market-orientated pricing
- production of small batches
- high investments in latest technology
- little traditional advertising
- in-house production
- finely-tuned logistics

After all, no matter which factor finally is responsible for Zara's outstanding performance, one thing is sure: every activity of the value chain, from electronic integration to logistics to manufacturing, is driven by customer satisfaction. This made Zara the world's fastest fashion retailer.

## 6.    Conclusion and outlook

Fast fashion retailers seek to quickly provide the newest trends for their fashion conscious buyers. They want to increase their cloth share in the customers' wardrobes (Mazaira et al., 2006). This leads to a strong increase in competitive pressure. However, companies are not only expected to manufacture fashion as fast as possible, but also to expand quickly. And although Zara already has about 1300 stores worldwide, the firm continues to open approximately 3 new stores per week (Inditex, 2009a). But industry experts think the company should rather slow down a bit. Fashion expert Allegra Piaggi warns: "Inditex's cost growth is exceeding its sales growth at the moment". According to him, a penetration of the markets that Zara entered so far would be advisable. (Allegra Piaggi, cited in Tiplady, 2006). But what if the European market once will be satisfied?

A glance at Inditex' financial report 2008 shows that the USA might be a tempting opportunity for Inditex. So far, Zara has solely few stores there and is the only Inditex format (Inditex 2009a). Therefore, the USA probably is the market with the biggest potential for growth. In the early 90s, Zara already looked towards the USA, but then decided to saturate the European market first before going overseas. Also, failed attempts of its main competitors Benetton and H&M, acted as a deterrent (Fuchs, 2005). However, in 1989, Zara finally decided to enter the US market and opened its first store in Manhattan. Unlike expansion in other countries, Zara tentative opened few stores a year. Today, Zara is represented with 41 stores. Not much considering the 330 Zara stores in Spain (Inditex 2009a). It seems that there is still plenty of space for the Spanish fashion retailer to expand.

Notwithstanding this fact and the more than satisfying actual development, it will be a big challenge to keep its business on a successful track. Questions such as "Are we able to cope with the complexity of managing multiple chains without compromising the excellence of individual ones?" "Should we start up or acquire additional chains?" Or simply: "What do we have to do to stay as successful as we are?" arise.

However, the answers to these and other questions are still written in the stars. The only thing that is certain by now is that Amancio Ortega managed to build a fashion empire that is spread all over the world. And even in these harsh times of economic recession, Zara's sales

figures are increasing steadily so that some might wonder how many more millions Zara will make before "getting into the cemetery of European retailers" (Fuchs, 2005).

# Appendix

## Appendix I: Inditex concepts

| Zara (Kiddy's Class) | Pull and Bear | Massimo Dutti | Bershka |
|---|---|---|---|
| 72 countries (5) | 39 countries | 38 countries | 40 countries |
| 1.292 stores (228) | 583 stores | 470 stores | 571 stores |
| business line casual line | casual, laid-back clothing | sophisticated urban fashions & casual wear | Tees, jeans, casual and urban wear |

| Stradivarius | Oysho | Zara Home | Uterqüe |
|---|---|---|---|
| 31 countries | 23 countries | 25 countries | 3 countries |
| 456 stores | 374 stores | 239 stores | 31 stores |
| International fashion with cutting-edge design | women's lingerie, informal clothes | home furnishings | accessories, textiles and leather garments |

Source:   Inditex (2009b)

**Appendix II: Zara's (Inditex) product positioning**

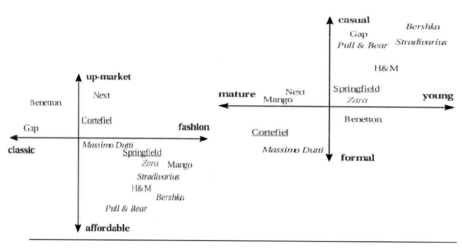

Source:   Fraiman et al. (2002)

**Appendix III: Sample Zara Price Tags**

| Country | Relative Price Level |
|---|---|
| Spain | 100% |
| United Kingdom | 151% |
| Denmark | 153% |
| Poland | 158% |
| Cyprus | 136% |
| Lebanon | 152% |
| Kuwait | 171% |
| Saudi Arabia | 170% |
| Bahrain | 170% |
| Qatar | 160% |
| Canada | 178% |
| USA | 209% |
| Mexico | 164% |
| Venezuela | 147% |
| Japan | 231% |

Source:   Ghemanwat and Nueno, (2006)

**Appendix IV: Zara's market cycle**

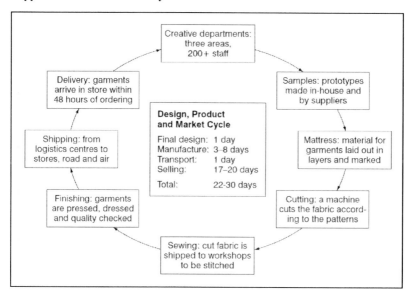

Source: Fernie, J. and Sparks, L. (2004)

**Appendix V: Inditex concepts**

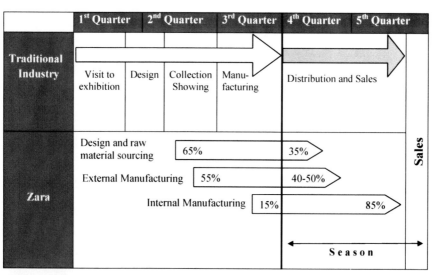

Source: Own illustration. Data adopted from Ghemawat and Nueno (2006)

**Appendix VI: Zara's business system**

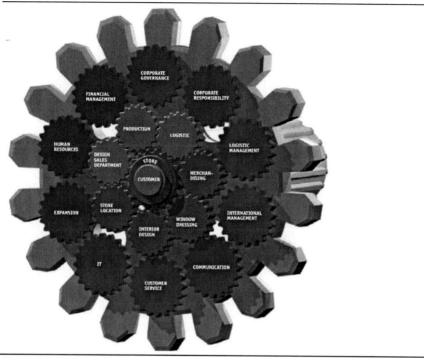

Source: Inditex (2008b)

**Appendix VII: Value chains for fashion retailers**

|  | Design | Manufacture | Store Management |
|---|---|---|---|
| Gap |  | Buys from external suppliers | Distribution |
| H&M |  | Buys from external suppliers | Distribution |
| Benetton |  | Brand Manufacture/ Management | Franchises |
| Inditex |  |  | Integrated Retailer |

Source: Mazaira et al., 2003 (modified)

**Appendix VIII: Data from Inditex and key international competitors**

| | Gap | H&M | Benetton | Inditex |
|---|---|---|---|---|
| **Operating Results * (€ Millions)** | | | | |
| **Net sales** | 12,518 | 6,524 | 1,765 | 6,741** |
| **Cost of sales** | 7,933 | 2,671 | 995 | 2,297 |
| **EBIT** | 1,363 | 1,403 | 157 | 1,093.6 |
| **Net Income** | 870 | 985 | 114 | 811 |
| **Number of Employees*** | 153,000 | 34,614 | 7,979 | 58,190 |
| **Number of Stores*** | 3,053 | 1,193 | 5,000 | 2,692 |
| **Global reach** | 6 countries | 34 countries | 120 countries | 73 countries |
| **Business model** | Partially vertically integrated, production is outsourced | Partially vertically integrated, production is outsourced | Highly vertically integrated | Highly vertically integrated |
| **Promotion** | 3% -3.5% of its turnover in advertising | 4% of its turnover in advertising | 4% of its turnover in advertising | 0.3% of its turnover in advertising |
| **Brand portfolio of parent** | Gap, BananaRepublic, Old Navy, and Piperlime | Single format | Sisley, Playlife and Killer Loop | Zara, Pull & Bear, Massimo Dutti, Bershka, Stradivarius, Oysho, Zara Home and Uterqüe |
| **Branding strategy** | Line extension | Multi-brand strategy | Multi-brand strategy | Line extension |

* Data refer to 2005

** The high net sales can be traced back to the fact that Inditex keeps its costs of sales low. This, in turn, can be traced back to the company's in-house production and its lower advertising expenses.

<u>Source:</u> Own illustration; compiled from annual reports.

# Bibliography

Ander W. N. and Stern, N. Z. (2004), *Winning at Retail. Developing a Sustained Model for Retail Success*, New Jersey: John Wiley & Sons.

AdAge (2006), 'Marketing 50 Awards',
<http://mediakit.adage.com/events/2007/Marketing50/Marketing50.htm>, accessed 24/02/09.

BBC (2004), 'Store Wars: Fast Fashion',
<http://news.bbc.co.uk/1/hi/business/3086669.stm>, accessed 20/04/09.

Benetton (2009), 'Corporate Website', www.benetton.com/, accessed 17/03/09.

Bowersox, D. J., Closs, D. J. and Stank, T. P. (2003), 'Understanding and mastering cross-enterprise collaborative supply chain management', *Supply Chain Management Review*, 7, no.4: 18-29.

Christopher, M., Lowson, R. and Peck, H. (2004), 'Creating agile supply chains in the fashion industry', *International Journal of Retail and Distribution Management*, 32, no.8: 367 – 376.

Coughlan, A. T., Anderson, E., Stern, L. W., and El-Ansary, A. I. (2006), *Marketing Channels*, 7th edn, Upper Saddle River, NJ: Prentice Hall.

D'Andrea, G. and Arnold, D. (2002), 'Zara', *Harvard Business School Case Study*, January 30th.

Day, G. S. (1994), 'The capabilities of market-driven organizations', *Journal of Marketing*, 58, no.4: 37-61.

Ferdows, K., Lewis, M.A. and Machuca, J. A. D. (2004), 'Rapid-fire fulfilment', *Harvard Business Review*, 82, no.11: 104-10.

Fernie, J., Moore, C., Lawrie, A. and Hallsworth, A. (1997), 'The internationalisation of the high fashion brand: the case of central London', *Journal of Product and Brand Management*, 6, no.3: 151-162.

Fernie, J. (1994), 'Quick response: an international perspective', *International Journal of Physical Distribution and Logistics Management*, 22, no.6: 38-46.

Fernie, J. and Sparks, L. (2004), 'Retail logistics: Changes and challenges', in Fernie, J. and Sparks, L. (eds), *Logistics and retail management: insights into current practice and trends from leading experts*, 2edn, London: Kogan Page.

Fraiman N., Singh M., Arrington L., and Paris C., (2002), *Zara*, New York: Columbia Business School Marketing Case.

Fuchs, D. (2005), 'Spanish Fashion Fleet Hitting Rough Seas', *The New York Times*, 20<sup>th</sup> August, <http://www.nytimes.com/iht/2005/08/20/business/IHT-20wbretail.html?pagewanted=2>, accessed 13/01/09.

Gap (2000), 'Corporate Website', <http://www.gap.com/>, accessed 07/03/09.

Gereffi, G. (2005), 'The global economy: organization, governance, and development. The global economy', in Smelser, N. J. and Swedberg, R. (eds.), *Handbook of Economic Sociology*, Princeton: University Press.

Ghemawat, P. and Nueno, J. L. (2006), 'Zara: Fast Fashion', *Harvard Business School Publishing*, Boston, MA.

Helft, M. (2002), Fashion Fast Forward. Business 2.0 3, no.5:61– 66.

Heller, R. (2001), 'Inside Zara', *Forbes*, New York, NY .

H&M (2009), 'Corporate Website', <http://www.hm.com/gb/>, accessed 03/03/09.

Hussein, R. T. and Al-Hour, B. M. (2009), 'The Impact of Market Orientation on Business Organizations' Performance. The Case of Jordan', *Journal of International Marketing and Marketing Research*, 34, no.1: 19-44.

Inditex (2009a), 'FY2008 RESULTS', http://www.inditex.com/en/shareholders_and_investors/investor_relations/quarterly_results, accessed 24/02/09.

Inditex (2009b), 'Zara', <http://www.inditex.com/en/who_we_are/concepts/zara>, accessed 21/03/09.

Inditex (2008a), 'Press kit', http://www.inditex.com/en/press/information/press_kit>, accessed 27/02/09.

Inditex (2008b), 'Annual Report 2007', <http://www.inditex.com/en/shareholders_and_investors/investor_relations/annual_re Ports>, accessed 19/04/09.

Keeley, G. and Clark, A. (2008), Zara overtakes Gap to become world's largest clothing retailer', The Guardian, 11th August, <http://www.guardian.co.uk/business/2008/aug/11/zara.gap.fashion>, accessed 12/02/09.

Kumar, N. and Steenkamp, J-B. E. M. (2007), 'Private label strategy: how to meet the store brand challenge', *Harvard Business School Press*, Cambrige, MA.

Kumar, N. & Linguri, S. (2006). 'Fashion sense', *Business Strategy Review*, 17, no.2: 80-84.

Langerak, F., Hultink, E. J., and Robben, H. (2004), 'The impact of market orientation, product advantage, and launch proficiency on new product performance and organizational performance', *Journal of Product Innovation Management*, 21, no.2: 79–94.

Lincoln, K and Thomassen, L. (2008), *Private Label: Turning the Retail Brand Threat Into Your Biggest Opportunity*, London, Kogan Page.

Mazaira, A., González, E. and Avendaño, R. (2003), 'The role of market orientation on company performance through the development of sustainable competitive advantage: the Inditex-Zara case', *Marketing Intelligence and Planning*, 21, no.4: 220-229.

Monllor, C. (2001), *Zarapolis: La historia secreta de un imperio de la moda*, Barcelona: Ediciones del Bronce.

Mossinkoff, M. R. H. and Stockert, A. M. (2008), 'Electronic integration in the apparel industry: the Charles Vögele case', *Journal of Fashion Marketing and Management*, 12, no.1: 90-104.

McAfee, A., Dessain, V. and Sjoman, A. (2004), 'Zara: IT for Fast Fashion', *Harvard Business School Publishing*, Boston, MA.

Narver, J. C. and Slater, S. (1990), 'The effect of a market orientation on business profitability', *Journal of Marketing*, 54, no.4: 20-35.

Nobukaza, J. A., Fernie, J. and Toshikazu, H. (2004), Market orientation and supply chain management in the fashion industry, in Fernie, J. and Sparks, J.(eds), 'Logistics and retail management: insights into current practice and trends from leading experts', 2nd edn, London: Kogan Page.

Prahalad, C. K. and Ramaswamy, V. (2004), *The future of competition: co-creating unique value with customers*, Harvard: Business School Press.

Reinach, S. S. (2005), China and Italy: Fast Fahion versus prêt a porter – towards a new culture of Fashion, *Fashion Theory*, 9,no.1: 43-56.

Singh, S. and Ranchhod, A. (2004), 'Market orientation and customer satisfaction: Evidence from British machine tool industry', *Industrial Marketing Management* 33, no.2: 135-144.

Sull, D. and Turconi, S. (2008), 'Fast fashion lessons', *Business Strategy Review*, 19, no.2: 4 – 11.

Tagliabue, J. (2003), 'Spanish Fashion chain Zara rivals gap by operating like dell', *New York Times*, 9 June.

The Economist (2005), 'The future of fast fashion: Inditex', *The Economist*, 375, no. 8431: p. 63.

Tiplady, R. (2006), 'Zara: Taking the Lead in Fast-Fashion', BusinessWeek, 4th April, < http://www.businessweek.com/globalbiz/content/apr2006/gb20060404_167078.htm>, accessed 21/04/09.

Tokatli, N. (2008), 'Global sourcing: insights from the global clothing industry – the case of Zara, a fast fashion retailer', *Journal of Economic Geography*, 8, no.1: 21-38.

Tungate, M. (2005), *Fashion Brands: Branding Styles from Armani to Zara*, London and Sterling, VA: Kogan Page.

Walters, D. (2006), Effectiveness and Efficiency: the role of demand chain management, *The International Journal of Logistics Management*, 17, no.1: 75-94.

Lightning Source UK Ltd.
Milton Keynes UK
UKOW05f0242221013

219515UK00001B/213/P